"COME, MY CHILDREN, LISTEN TO ME; I WILL TEACH YOU THE FEAR OF THE LORD" - PSALM 34:11

FEAR
OF THE
LORD

DARIUS GOOD

FROM THE AUTHOR OF *"UNLOCKING GODLY WISDOM: SOLOMON'S 7 PILLARS OF WISDOM"*

FEAR OF THE LORD

Copyright ©2022 Darius Good

All rights reserved

Published by Darius Good for Good Treasure Ministries

All rights reserved. This book or any portion thereof may not be reproduced, distributed, or transmitted in any form or by any means, including photocopying, recording, and other electronic or mechanical methods, or used in any manner whatsoever, without the express written permission of the publisher, except for the use of brief quotations in a book review.

TABLE OF CONTENTS:

CHAPTER 1	A Man After God's Heart	1
CHAPTER 2	A Psalmist Heart	5
CHAPTER 3	Fear Must Be Taught	10
CHAPTER 4	God's Treasure	17
CHAPTER 5	Choose Today	26
CHAPTER 6	Lesson 1	30
CHAPTER 7	Peter Teaches the Fear of the Lord	47
CHAPTER 8	Paul's Teachings on the Godly Fear	51
CHAPTER 9	Lesson 2	54
CHAPTER 10	The Beginning of Knowledge	63
CHAPTER 11	If Any Lack Wisdom	73
CHAPTER 12	The Mind of a King	78
CHAPTER 13	For Them that Fear Him	89
CHAPTER 14	Godly Fear	95
CHAPTER 15	Learn to Fear	98

CHAPTER 1

A MAN AFTER GOD'S HEART

In the Bible, David is one of the most iconic individuals. God was so pleased with David that He vowed that Jesus would come through his bloodline. David's life has been the focus of many Sunday sermons, as he exemplified a man that was far from perfect, yet was described by God as a man after His own heart.

1 Samuel 13:14 (KJV)
But now thy kingdom shall not continue: **the LORD hath sought him a man after his own heart***, and the LORD hath commanded him [to be] captain over his people, because thou hast not kept [that] which the LORD commanded thee.*

In 1 Samuel 13, Samuel is telling king Saul that God had rejected him. This moment reveals why Saul was ultimately disqualified as an heir of Christ but even after David sinned, he was not. Saul on several occasions disobeyed God. He was given instructions by God and he would deviate from the plan. When Saul decided to perform the burnt offering, which could only be performed by a priest, Saul had crossed the line. God was going to establish Saul's kingdom forever. Jesus would have come through his line. In doing so, Saul's bloodline would have been eternal because king Jesus lives forever more. He is the resurrected King.

1 Samuel 13:13 (KJV)
And Samuel said to Saul, Thou hast done foolishly: thou hast not kept the commandment of the LORD thy God, which he commanded thee: for now would the LORD have established thy kingdom upon Israel for ever.

In moments of correction, Saul never repented. He always blamed others (blame shifted) or found an excuse for his disobedience.

1 Samuel 13:11-12 (KJV)
11 And Samuel said, What hast thou done? And Saul said, Because I saw that the people were scattered from me, and [that] thou camest not within the days appointed, and [that] the Philistines gathered themselves together at Michmash;

12 Therefore said I, The Philistines will come down now upon me to Gilgal, and I have not made supplication unto the LORD: I forced myself therefore, and offered a burnt offering.

Notice David's response when God sent the prophet Nathan to correct him for killing Uriah and taking his wife. David's response was, "I have sinned."

2 Samuel 12:13 (KJV)
And David said unto Nathan, I have sinned against the LORD. And Nathan said unto David, The LORD also hath put away thy sin; thou shalt not die.

David made mistakes in his life. Bad ones. But he was always willing to correct them. He desired to live a life pleasing to God. Psalms 51 reveals the prayer and heart of David when God confronted him. David had a repentant heart. He accepted responsibility for his actions and decisions. And he accepted the consequence. Psalms 51 reveals David's prayer and attitude following God's correction.

Psalms 51:10 (KJV)
Create in me a clean heart, O God; and renew a right spirit within me.

Psalms 51:17 (KJV)
The sacrifices of God [are] a broken spirit: a broken and a contrite heart, O God, thou wilt not despise.

David's heart was broken (contrite) and he cried to the Lord to be cleansed. The sin David committed required death as payment. The wages (payment) for sin is death. God spared David's life because of their covenant but the baby's life was not spared. It also produced acts of violence throughout David's house, costing the lives of several of David's children. David also lost his wives. What was done in secret, was now rewarded to David publicly in front of the entire nation.

2 Samuel 12:10-12 (KJV)
10 *Now therefore the sword shall never depart from thine house; because thou hast despised me, and hast taken the wife of Uriah the Hittite to be thy wife.*

11 *Thus saith the LORD, Behold, I will raise up evil against thee out of thine own house, and I will take thy wives before thine eyes, and give [them] unto thy neighbour, and he shall lie with thy wives in the sight of this sun.*

12 *For thou didst [it] secretly: but I will do this thing before all Israel, and before the sun.*

Despite David's imperfections, David was a man after God's own heart. Why is this? Most teachings I have heard say that because David was a worshipper. David loved God. He was a praiser and a worshipper and David is attributed with writing the majority of the book of Psalms. However, the book of Psalms explains the key to David's mindset and heart. David feared the Lord.

CHAPTER 2

A PSALMIST HEART

FEAR OF THE LORD

Throughout the scriptures, you will find several phrases: "the fear of the Lord", "the fear of God", or "godly fear". In the book of Psalms, the scriptures mention "not being afraid" or "I will not fear." This is a different type of fear. These statements are not connected to the fear of the Lord. Listed below are the scriptures that reference the fear of the Lord.

This was David's heart. This was David's mindset. Though every chapter in Psalms was not written by David, you see the "fear of the Lord" from the beginning of Psalms till the end.

Psalm 2:11 (KJV)
Serve the LORD with fear, and rejoice with trembling.

Psalm 15:4 (KJV)
In whose eyes a vile person is contemned; but he honoureth them that fear the LORD. [He that] sweareth to [his own] hurt, and changeth not.

Psalm 19:9 (KJV)
The fear of the LORD [is] clean, enduring for ever: the judgments of the LORD [are] true [and] righteous altogether.

Psalm 22:23 (KJV)
Ye that fear the LORD, praise him; all ye the seed of Jacob, glorify him; and fear him, all ye the seed of Israel.

Psalm 25:14 (KJV)
The secret of the LORD [is] with them that fear him; and he will shew them his covenant.

Psalm 33:8 (KJV)
Let all the earth fear the LORD: let all the inhabitants of the world stand in awe of him.

Psalm 33:18 (KJV)
Behold, the eye of the LORD [is] upon them that fear him, upon them that hope in his mercy;

Psalm 34:7 (KJV)
The angel of the LORD encampeth round about them that fear him, and delivereth them.

Psalm 34:9 (KJV)
O fear the LORD, ye his saints: for [there is] no want to them that fear him.

Psalm 34:11 (KJV)
Come, ye children, hearken unto me: I will teach you the fear of the LORD.

Psalm 40:3 (KJV)
And he hath put a new song in my mouth, [even] praise unto our God: many shall see [it], and fear, and shall trust in the LORD.

Psalm 64:9 (KJV)
And all men shall fear, and shall declare the work of God; for they shall wisely consider of his doing.

Psalm 66:16 (KJV)
Come [and] hear, all ye that fear God, and I will declare what he hath done for my soul.

FEAR OF THE LORD

Psalm 67:7 (KJV)
God shall bless us; and all the ends of the earth shall fear him.

Psalm 86:11 (KJV)
Teach me thy way, O LORD; I will walk in thy truth: unite my heart to fear thy name.

Psalm 96:9 (KJV)
O worship the LORD in the beauty of holiness: fear before him, all the earth.

Psalm 103:13 (KJV)
Like as a father pitieth [his] children, [so] the LORD pitieth them that fear him.

Psalm 103:17 (KJV)
But the mercy of the LORD [is] from everlasting to everlasting upon them that fear him, and his righteousness unto children's children;

Psalm 111:10 (KJV)
The fear of the LORD [is] the beginning of wisdom: a good understanding have all they that do [his commandments]: his praise endureth for ever.

Psalm 115:11 (KJV)
Ye that fear the LORD, trust in the LORD: he [is] their help and their shield.

Psalm 115:13 (KJV)
He will bless them that fear the LORD, [both] small and great.

Psalm 118:4 (KJV)
Let them now that fear the LORD say, that his mercy [endureth] for ever.

Psalm 135:20 (KJV)
Bless the LORD, O house of Levi: ye that fear the LORD, bless the LORD.

Psalm 147:11 (KJV)
The LORD taketh pleasure in them that fear him, in those that hope in his mercy.

Before David died. His final words included the "fear of the Lord." He said those that are called to lead and rule, must rule in the fear of the Lord.

2 Samuel 23:1-3 (KJV)
1 Now these [be] the last words of David. David the son of Jesse said, and the man [who was] raised up on high, the anointed of the God of Jacob, and the sweet psalmist of Israel, said,
2 The Spirit of the LORD spake by me, and his word [was] in my tongue.
3 The God of Israel said, the Rock of Israel spake to me, He that ruleth over men [must be] just, **ruling in the fear of God.**

David lived his life in godly fear. He ruled the nation in the fear of the Lord. This means his life and ministry were governed by this mindset. God takes pleasure in those that fear Him.

CHAPTER 3

FEAR MUST BE TAUGHT

I heard someone say "fear means terror", so the fear of the Lord means to be in terror of God or be afraid of God. This type of fear is not what the fear of the Lord is.

There are different types of fears mentioned in the scriptures. Human fear, the fear of man, the fear of the Lord, the spirit of fear, and more. It's important to understand the fear of the Lord is not people being afraid of God.

God desires that we come to Him. In Him, there is no fear. God is love! He is perfect love.

1 John 4:18 (KJV)
There is no fear in love; but perfect love casteth out fear: because fear hath torment. He that feareth is not made perfect in love.

Even in our sins, God does not want us to be afraid of Him. He is not condemning. He loves the world. For this reason, He sent His son Jesus to die on the cross. As His children, we are called to be like Him: kind, tenderhearted, and forgiving.

Ephesians 4:32 (KJV)
And be ye kind one to another, tenderhearted, forgiving one another, ***even as God for Christ's sake hath forgiven you.***

God makes His rain fall on the just and the unjust. And His sun rises on the good and the evil. God is kind to the unthankful and to those that are evil. It is God's goodness that brings men to repentance.

FEAR OF THE LORD

Luke 6:35 (KJV)
But love ye your enemies, and do good, and lend, hoping for nothing again; and your reward shall be great, and ye shall be the children of the Highest: for **he is kind unto the unthankful and [to] the evil.**

I have heard many teach, "The fear of the Lord is honoring God." To hold God in high esteem and reverence Him, reverential fear.

Merriam-Webster dictionary defines the word fear as profound reverence and awe, especially toward God.

We can begin here with our understanding, but this is far from the depth of this concept. The children of Israel were required to learn the fear of the Lord. It had to be taught to them.

Psalm 34:11 (KJV)
Come, ye children, hearken unto me: I will teach you the fear of the LORD.

To teach something would mean there are layers to what the fear of the Lord is. It was taught to the entire nation. The children were required to learn it from their youth.

Deuteronomy 4:10 (KJV)
[Specially] the day that thou stoodest before the LORD thy God in Horeb, when the LORD said unto me, Gather me the people together, and I will make them hear my words, that they may learn to fear me all the days that they shall live upon the earth, and [that] they may teach their children.

Obadiah learned the fear of the Lord from his youth. He explained this to Elijah, hoping Elijah would keep his word and spare his life.

FEAR MUST BE TAUGHT

1 Kings 18:7-12 (KJV)

7 And as Obadiah was in the way, behold, Elijah met him: and he knew him, and fell on his face, and said, [Art] thou that my lord Elijah?

8 And he answered him, I [am]: go, tell thy lord, Behold, Elijah [is here].

9 And he said, What have I sinned, that thou wouldest deliver thy servant into the hand of Ahab, to slay me?

10 [As] the LORD thy God liveth, there is no nation or kingdom, whither my lord hath not sent to seek thee: and when they said, [He is] not [there]; he took an oath of the kingdom and nation, that they found thee not.

11 And now thou sayest, Go, tell thy lord, Behold, Elijah [is here].

12 And it shall come to pass, [as soon as] I am gone from thee, that the Spirit of the LORD shall carry thee whither I know not; and [so] when I come and tell Ahab, and he cannot find thee, he shall slay me: **but I thy servant fear the LORD from my youth.**

The king of Assyria had a priest come and teach them the fear of the Lord.

2 Kings 17:27-28 (KJV)

27 Then the king of Assyria commanded, saying, Carry thither one of the priests whom ye brought from thence; and let them go and dwell there, and let him teach them the manner of the God of the land.

28 Then one of the priests whom they had carried away from Samaria came and dwelt in Bethel, **and taught them how they should fear the LORD.**

Samuel told the nation of Israel that he would teach them the ways of God and the fear of the Lord after Saul was chosen to be king.

1 Samuel 12:23-25 (KJV)
23 Moreover as for me, God forbid that I should sin against the LORD in ceasing to pray for you: **but I will teach you the good and the right way:**
24 Only fear the LORD, *and serve him in truth with all your heart: for consider how great [things] he hath done for you.*
25 But if ye shall still do wickedly, ye shall be consumed, both ye and your king.

Psalm 86:11 (KJV)
Teach me thy way, O LORD; I will walk in thy truth: unite my heart to fear thy name.

David prayed and asked the Lord to teach him His ways. David was saying, show me your ways or your patterns. Show me your systems. Show me how it works and how I am to do it.

Next, David said, I will walk in God's truth. You can't walk if you don't know the way. So, the truth comes to reveal the way, and then you walk out God's instructions. If there are issues with the heart, you obey the instructions and shift your heart. This is a place where I have seen many people struggle. But the change of heart is a decision. This is called repentance. And repentance is not only a part of the prayer of salvation but also a continuous experience that produces growth and maturity. Repentance is to change the way one thinks for the better. It is repentance that causes us to go from one level to the next.

David's prayer was that God would "unite his heart to fear His name." To unite or join is the opposite of dividing. So, David was praying for an undivided heart. A heart that was wholeheartedly committed to fearing God. A pure heart.

The opposite of David's prayer is one who is double-minded. A double-minded person is unstable in all of their ways. They are relying on or vacillating between two systems, rather than one.

David is saying, that he will not be double-minded. His heart was not divided. He is relying on the principle of the fear of the Lord. He refused to follow or live by any other principle.

David was fully committed to learning the lesson of the fear of the Lord. He applied this understanding. This was the principle that David lived by from the point that he learned it until he died.

This means as David came to an understanding of what the fear of the Lord is, he made some life-changing decisions. I can't live that way anymore. I am going to live this way from now on.

The fear of the Lord requires you to tear down mindsets and establish new ones.

In Deuteronomy 4:10 (KJV) part of God's instructions was they were to apply this lesson of fearing Him all of the days of their lives. "That they may learn to fear me all the days that they shall live upon the earth…"

This lesson was not one that you learn, receive a passing grade, and move on. God required them to walk in this understanding until they died. It becomes who and what you are.

"Fear me all the days that they shall live upon the earth." This lesson taught them how to live.

The fear of the Lord teaches and shows you how to live.

God also required it to be taught to the next generation.

Deuteronomy 10:12 (KJV)
And now, Israel, what doth the LORD thy God require of thee, but to fear the LORD thy God, to walk in all his ways, and to love him, and to serve the LORD thy God with all thy heart and with all thy soul,

The fear of the Lord is a mindset and a lifestyle. It is a requirement if we are going to live a life pleasing to the Lord.

CHAPTER 4

GOD'S TREASURE

FEAR OF THE LORD

Psalm 111:10 says the fear of the Lord is the beginning of wisdom. Proverbs 1:7 says the fear of the Lord is the beginning of knowledge.

Psalm 111:10 (KJV)
The fear of the LORD [is] the <u>beginning</u> of wisdom: *a good understanding have all they that do [his commandments]: his praise endureth for ever.*

Proverbs 1:7 (KJV)
The fear of the LORD [is] the <u>beginning</u> of knowledge: *[but] fools despise wisdom and instruction.*

The word beginning is *rē'šîṯ* it means the first, in place, time, order or rank, chief, head, top.

The fear of the Lord is a principle. It is the primary source. It is the first step. The prerequisite to the deep things of God. Isaiah 33:6 calls it "God's treasure." It is the most valuable part of the equation of a successful godly life.

The fear of the Lord is the first principle, the foundation, the fundamental principle of the system of wisdom and knowledge, and more.

Before we understand wisdom or knowledge, we must have a solid grasp on the fear of the Lord because it is the foundation. Wisdom is built on the fear of the Lord. Knowledge is built on the fear of the Lord.

> *Let's look at all the systems that the fear of the Lord is connected to and its effects.*

Psalm 34:7 (KJV)

The angel of the LORD *encampeth round about them that fear him, and delivereth them.*

➢ Angelic protection

Psalm 34:9

O fear the LORD*, ye his saints: for there is no want to them that fear him.*

➢ No wants (the Lord is my shepherd…)

Psalm 103:11

For as the heaven is high above the earth, so great is his mercy toward them that fear him.

➢ Mercy

Psalm 147:11 (KJV)

The LORD *taketh pleasure in them that fear him, in those that hope in his mercy.*

➢ Pleasure (God takes pleasure/delights)

Psalm 103:13 (KJV)

Like as a father pitieth his children, so the LORD *pitieth them that fear him.*

➢ Pitieth (love, compassion, kind)

Psalm 145:19 (KJV)

He will fulfill the desire of them that fear Him; He also will hear their cry and will save them.

- ➢ **Fulfills desires (favor)**
- ➢ **Prayer (hears their cry)**

Isaiah 33:6 (KJV)
And wisdom and knowledge shall be the stability of thy times, [and] strength of salvation: the fear of the LORD [is] his treasure.

Isaiah 33:6 (NET)
He is your constant source of stability; he abundantly provides safety and great wisdom; he gives all this to those who fear him.

Isaiah 33:6 (NIV)
He will be the sure foundation for your times, a rich store of salvation and wisdom and knowledge; the fear of the LORD is the key to this treasure.

- ➢ **Stability (of time)**
- ➢ **Salvation (safety and strength)**
- ➢ **Wisdom**
- ➢ **Knowledge**

Psalm 5:7 (KJV)
But as for me, I will come [into] thy house in the multitude of thy mercy: [and] in thy fear will I worship toward thy holy temple.

Psalm 111:10 (KJV)
The fear of the LORD [is] the beginning of wisdom: a good understanding have all they that do [his commandments]: his praise endureth for ever.

Proverbs 1:7 (KJV)

The fear of the LORD [is] the beginning of knowledge: [but] fools despise wisdom and instruction.

Proverbs 15:33 (KJV)

The fear of the LORD [is] the instruction of wisdom; and before honour [is] humility.

Psalm 15:4 (KJV)

In whose eyes a vile person is contemned; but he honoureth them that fear the LORD. [He that] sweareth to [his own] hurt, and changeth not.

- **Worship**
- **Understanding**
- **Honor**
- **Humility**
- **Instruction (of wisdom)**

Psalm 22:23

Ye that fear the LORD, praise him; all ye the seed of Jacob, glorify him; and fear him, all ye the seed of Israel.

- **Praise**

2 Corinthians 7:1 (KJV)

Having therefore these promises, dearly beloved, let us cleanse ourselves from all filthiness of the flesh and spirit, perfecting holiness in the fear of God.

- ➢ **Washed, cleansed**
- ➢ **Holiness**

Deuteronomy 10:12 (KJV)
And now, Israel, what doth the LORD thy God require of thee, but to fear the LORD thy God, to walk in all his ways, and to love him, and to serve the LORD thy God with all thy heart and with all thy soul,

Deuteronomy 13:4 (KJV)
Ye shall walk after the LORD your God, and fear him, and keep his commandments, and obey his voice, and ye shall serve him, and cleave unto him.

- ➢ **Walking in God's ways**
- ➢ **Keep God's commandments**
- ➢ **Obedience (obeying God's voice)**
- ➢ **Love the Lord**
- ➢ **Serve (service to) God**

Psalm 115:13-14 (KJV)
13 He will bless them that fear the Lord, both small and great.

14 The LORD shall increase you more and more, you and your children.

- ➢ **Increase**

Acts 9:31 (KJV)
Then the church throughout Judea, Galilee and Samaria enjoyed a time of peace and was strengthened. Living in the fear of

the Lord and encouraged by the Holy Spirit, it increased in numbers.

- ➢ **Peace**

2 Samuel 23:3 (KJV)
The God of Israel said, the Rock of Israel spake to me, He that ruleth over men must be just [righteous], ruling in the fear of God.

- ➢ **Rulership (to rule, exercise, and have dominion, reign)**
- ➢ **Justice**

Hebrews 12:28 (KJV)
Wherefore we receiving a kingdom which cannot be moved, let us have grace, whereby we may serve God acceptably with reverence and godly fear:

- ➢ **Grace (God's ability, empowerment)**
- ➢ **Reverence**

Psalm 61:5 (CSB)
God, you have heard my vows; you have given a heritage to those who fear your name.

- ➢ **Vows**
- ➢ **Heritage (inheritance)**

Psalm 25:14 (KJV)
The secret of the LORD is with them that fear him; and he will shew them his covenant.

- **Secrets**
- **Covenants**

Ephesians 5:21-22

21 Submitting yourselves one to another in the fear of God.

22 Wives, submit yourselves unto your own husbands, as unto the Lord

Submission to one another must be done in the fear of the Lord. And wives are to simply submit to their husbands, but this submission is to be done in godly fear. And the husband must be submitted to God, in godly fear.

- **Submission (to those in leadership, to one another, in marriage)**

Malachi 4:2 (KJV)
But unto you that fear my name shall the Sun of righteousness arise with healing in his wings; and ye shall go forth, and grow up as calves of the stall.

- **Healing**

Deuteronomy 6:2 (KJV)
so that you, your children and their children after them may fear the LORD your God as long as you live by keeping all his decrees and commands that I give you, and so that you may enjoy long life.

Proverbs 10:27 (KJV)
The fear of the LORD adds length to life, but the years of the wicked are cut short.

- **Long lifestyle (enjoyable life)**
- **Adds days to our life**

Acts 10:35 (KJV)
But in every nation he that feareth him, and worketh righteousness, is accepted with him.

- **Righteousness (the just, justification)**

The fear of the Lord is the first principle of everything mentioned above. There are so many systems in God's kingdom connected to the fear of the Lord. There are so many principles, functions, operating systems, and kingdom lifestyle requirements that are built on this principle. The fear of the Lord is the most important treasure (commodity) in God's kingdom. The fear of the Lord unlocks the relationship God desires to have with us. It is the key to the fullness of His plan for our lives. A successful life (by Godly standards) is unobtainable without the fear of the Lord.

Through the fear of the Lord, David was able to see that God did not desire the blood of animals. David desired to know God's heart. It was the closeness of this relationship that revealed to David that God wanted people's hearts. David saw this, thousands of years before the New Testament covenant was established. David saw behind the veil. God showed David His secrets and explained His mysteries to David because he feared the Lord. This is what made David a man after God's own heart.

CHAPTER 5

CHOOSE TODAY

Deuteronomy 28:58 (KJV)

58 If thou wilt not observe to do all the words of this law that are written in this book, that thou mayest ***fear this glorious and fearful name, THE LORD THY GOD;***

God required the entire nation to learn to fear Him. In Deuteronomy 28, God told them what would happen if they did not fear Him. This passage is connecting fearing the Lord with obeying and keeping His commandments. By breaking the commandments because they did not fear the Lord, the Lord revealed the consequence of this decision.

Deuteronomy 28:58-68 (NIV)

58 If you do not carefully follow all the words of this law, which are written in this book, and do not revere this glorious and awesome name--the LORD your God--

59 the LORD will send fearful plagues on you and your descendants, harsh and prolonged disasters, and severe and lingering illnesses.

60 He will bring on you all the diseases of Egypt that you dreaded, and they will cling to you.

61 The LORD will also bring on you every kind of sickness and disaster not recorded in this Book of the Law, until you are destroyed.

62 You who were as numerous as the stars in the sky will be left but few in number, because you did not obey the LORD your God.

63 Just as it pleased the LORD to make you prosper and increase in number, so it will please him to ruin and destroy you. You will be uprooted from the land you are entering to possess.

64 Then the LORD will scatter you among all nations, from one end of the earth to the other. There you will worship other gods--gods of wood and stone, which neither you nor your ancestors have known.

65 *Among those nations you will find no repose, no resting place for the sole of your foot. There the LORD will give you an anxious mind, eyes weary with longing, and a despairing heart.*

66 *You will live in constant suspense, filled with dread both night and day, never sure of your life.*

67 *In the morning you will say, "If only it were evening!" and in the evening, "If only it were morning!"--because of the terror that will fill your hearts and the sights that your eyes will see.*

68 *The LORD will send you back in ships to Egypt on a journey I said you should never make again. There you will offer yourselves for sale to your enemies as male and female slaves, but no one will buy you.*

In spite of this very vivid explanation of what they would experience if they did not fear the Lord, the Israelites still backslid repeatedly. They suffered many of the things God said they would.

Many read statements like Deuteronomy 28:58-68 and view God as an angry God. He punishes people when they're disobedient and makes them suffer. But the outcome people suffer is a result of disobedience. David's prayer to the Lord was to teach him His way.

Psalms 86:11 (KJV)
Teach me thy way, O LORD; I will walk in thy truth: unite my heart to fear thy name.

The fear of the Lord requires obedience, following instructions, learning, and keeping the way of God. If man obeys the ways of God, they will not suffer. If they will remain on the road of righteousness laid out by God, they will remain safe. There's danger off the path. When men stray from the road and do not follow the instructions, then they experience the things God warned them of. God does not control people. Every person has a will. But people must choose to be obedient. If God says there is danger up ahead, it is on the person to listen.

Proverbs 14: 27 (KJV)
The fear of the LORD [is] a fountain of life, to depart from the snares of death.

Psalms 18:30 (NLT)
God's way is perfect. All the LORD's promises prove true. He is a shield for all who look to him for protection.

We must keep and follow God's way. His system, course, road, steps, manners, conduct, pattern, and responses are what produce life. We only know what to do, how to do it, when to do it and why we are doing it because of God's word. His word tells me the next step.

Psalms 119:105 (KJV)
NUN. Thy word [is] a lamp unto my feet, and a light unto my path.

The outcome is in our hands. Our success is in our hands. God is the cheat code to our success. Those that listen and obey will live. Those that do not, have chosen their own path.

Psalms 119:109 (KJV)
My soul [is] continually in my hand: yet do I not forget thy law.

Deuteronomy 30:19 (NLT)
"Today I have given you the choice between life and death, between blessings and curses. Now I call on heaven and earth to witness the choice you make. Oh, that you would choose life, so that you and your descendants might live!

The choice is yours!

CHAPTER 6

LESSON 1

The fear of the Lord is a principle.

Principle:

1: (a) a comprehensive and fundamental law, doctrine

(b): a rule or code of conduct

The scriptures reveal in several different passages what the fear of the Lord is. When we put it all together, we have a complete picture of this law.

1. Keeping God's commandments (law)

Deuteronomy 6: (KJV)
*1 Now these [are] the **commandments, the statutes, and the judgments**, which the LORD your God commanded to teach you, that ye might do [them] in the land whither ye go to possess it:*

*2 That thou mightest fear the LORD thy God, to **keep all his statutes and his commandments**, which I command thee, thou, and thy son, and thy son's son, all the days of thy life; and that thy days may be prolonged.*

Deuteronomy 6:1-2 instructs us to learn and do God's commandments, statutes, and judgments.

Nehemiah 9:13-14 (KJV)
13 Thou camest down also upon mount Sinai, and spakest with them from heaven, and gavest them right judgments, and true laws, good statutes and commandments:

14 *And madest known unto them thy holy sabbath, and* **commandedst them precepts, statutes, and laws,** *by the hand of Moses thy servant:*

At Mount Sinai, when Moses returned with the Ten Commandments, he taught the people right judgments, true laws, good statutes, and commandments. In Nehemiah 9:13, we see that precepts were given to them at that time as well.

Ordinances were also given to the people. If they profaned the ordinances of God, the penalty was death, as it was with the laws of God.

Leviticus 22:9 (KJV)
They shall therefore keep mine ordinance, lest they bear sin for it, and die therefore, if they profane it: I the LORD do sanctify them.

So, the fear of the Lord is the keeping of God's commandments, statutes, judgment (ordinances), and precepts.

Commandments
A commandment is an order or a charge to be followed and observed. These were instructions given by God that had to be observed. Those that broke God's commandments were punished by death (Leviticus 24:10-23). Sin offerings were only offered for sins committed through ignorance, never on purpose (Leviticus 4).

Statues
The decrees or requirements describing how to live in obedience to God. It is a civil decree. It prescribes what we are to do. And there are boundaries or limitations on what we cannot do. For example, how to observe the sabbath, which was an Old Testament requirement.

Judgments (ordinances)

Judgment was the way disputes were handled. Moses established a court system that would listen to and judge disputes according to the Mosaic Law. Every town had a judge to hear the cases. The more difficult cases were passed up to the elders. If it could not be resolved on that level, then Moses would hear the case. The innocent was vindicated and the guilty was responsible for restitution.

Deuteronomy 25:1 (KJV)
If there be a controversy between men, and they come unto judgment, that [the judges] may judge them; then they shall justify the righteous, and condemn the wicked.

Those that rejected the sentencing and verdict of the priests or the judges, were put to death.

Deuteronomy 17:12 (NLT)
Anyone arrogant enough to reject the verdict of the judge or of the priest who represents the LORD your God must die. In this way, you will purge the evil from Israel.

Precepts

A precept is a commandment or direction given as a rule of action or conduct. It's an injunction as to moral conduct.

God told them in Deuteronomy 6 they were to teach God's commandments, statutes, judgments, and precepts to their son and son's son. This means each generation was to learn the laws of God and keep them. The laws were taught in every Israelite home. And the priest would teach the laws to the nation. No one in the nation of Israel was ignorant of the law. If a law was broken through ignorance, it meant that the person did not have any intention of breaking the law. For example, an axe head flew off killing a person by accident. For laws that were broken on purpose, the penalty was death.

God also required each king to write their own copy of the law. Each king hand wrote their own book of the law. They were required to read the law all the days of their life so that they would learn to fear the Lord and keep the law and statutes of God.

Deuteronomy 17:
18 And it shall be, when he sitteth upon the throne of his kingdom, that he shall write him a copy of this law in a book out of [that which is] before the priests the Levites:

19 And it shall be with him, and he shall read therein all the days of his life: that he may learn to fear the LORD his God, to keep all the words of this law and these statutes, to do them:

Under our New Testament covenant, we are no longer under the law. We are under grace. This does not mean the Mosaic law has been done away with. Jesus stated that he did not come to do away with the law. But He did reveal how it is to be fulfilled. One is by love and the other way is by faith.

Galatians 5:14 (KJV)
For all the law is fulfilled in one word, [even] in this; Thou shalt love thy neighbour as thyself.

Galatians 3:11 (KJV)
But that no man is justified [made righteous] by the law in the sight of God, [it is] evident: for, The just [righteous] shall live by faith.

We are made righteous through faith. Faith comes by hearing God's word. This means God must speak first, we hear and believe. We are to believe God's word until we receive what He has promised. We must have faith (belief) and doubt not.

Galatians 3:6 (KJV)
Even as Abraham believed God, and it was accounted to him for righteousness.

Matthew 21:21 (KJV)
Jesus answered and said unto them, Verily I say unto you, If ye **have faith, and doubt not...**

By believing and obedience (faith without works is dead) we will receive what God has said. This is the lifestyle of faith.

Romans 4:20-21 (KJV)
20 *He staggered not at the promise of God through unbelief; but was strong in faith, giving glory to God;*
21 *And being fully persuaded that, what he had promised, he was able also to perform.*

This is how we walk by faith and not by sight. If God promised it, He can perform it!

Also, lifestyle is important in keeping God's commandments. Just as sin offerings could only be offered for sins committed in ignorance, we cannot continue in our former ways of life. We must come into truth and light and remain in the light. Once we receive knowledge of the truth, we cannot continue to sin. Jesus' blood cannot be continuously offered for our sins. If we live a life of habitual sin, we trample the blood of Jesus underfoot and are guilty of treating His blood as being unholy.

Hebrews 10:26 (KJV)
For if we sin wilfully after that we have received the knowledge of the truth, there remaineth no more sacrifice for sins,

Hebrews 10:29 (NIV)
How much more severely do you think someone deserves to be punished who has trampled the Son of God underfoot, who has treated as an unholy thing the blood of the covenant that sanctified them, and who has insulted the Spirit of grace?

A lifestyle of obedience and faith does not mean that we forget about the law. We fulfill the law when we love one another and when we have faith, but this liberty (no more blood sacrifices, feasts, oblations, offerings according to the law of Moses) does not allow us to live a life of sin.

Romans 3:31 (New Living Translation)
31 Well then, if we emphasize faith, does this mean that we can forget about the law? Of course not! In fact, only when we have faith do we truly fulfill the law.

2. Tithing
3. Worship and service

Deuteronomy 14:23 (KJV)
And thou shalt eat before the LORD thy God, in the place which he shall choose to place his name there, the tithe of thy corn, of thy wine, and of thine oil, and the firstlings of thy herds and of thy flocks; **that thou mayest learn to fear the LORD thy God always.**

Deuteronomy 14:23 (NLT)

*Bring this tithe to the designated place of **worship**--the place the LORD your God chooses for his name to be honored--and eat it there in his presence. **This applies to your tithes** of grain, new wine, olive oil, and the firstborn males of your flocks and herds. **Doing this will teach you always to fear the LORD your God.***

Tithe comes from the word to ʿāśar and it means: tithe, take the tenth part of, give a tithe, take a tithe. The root word ʿāśar means to accumulate, to grow, and make rich.

They were required to bring God a portion of their increase.

Deuteronomy 14:22 (KJV)

Thou shalt truly tithe all the increase of thy seed, that the field bringeth forth year by year.

Worship to a deity is never determined by man. God reveals how He is to be worshipped. Many people struggle with the concept of tithing. There are many debates on if tithing is a part of the New Testament covenant. The fear of the Lord is an Old Testament concept, but it is also taught in the New Testament. The apostle Paul and Peter taught about the fear of the Lord. My suggestion would be to follow the instructions as given first. Give ten percent. If the Lord tells you otherwise, then follow His voice. But too often, people like to alter the recipe to the cake before mastering the recipe. Let's stick to the instructions so we can receive what the Lord has promised us through His word.

Tithe was not only given to the priest. There was a tithe also given to the stranger (foreigners), orphans, and widows (Deuteronomy 26:12). The concept is to give. Give to God and give to others. Jesus said in Luke 6:38, "Give and it shall be give unto you..."

In the Old Testament, God instructed man how to worship Him. Man was required to follow specific instructions. They built alters. First, the location of where the altar was to be built was specified by God and not man. Second, the materials used were determined by God. The altars were made of stone and no tool could touch the stones. Building an altar required time, effort, and planning. The altar had to be built stone on top of stone. They were told what they could not do. They could not make images of God out of gold or silver. They could not decide what they would bring to God as an offering. God told them what animal to offer and the specifications (sex, first born, age, no blemishes, etc.) So, the sacrifice itself was determined by God.

Exodus 20:23-25 (KJV)
23 Ye shall not make with me gods of silver, neither shall ye make unto you gods of gold. 24 An altar of earth thou shalt make unto me, and shalt sacrifice thereon thy burnt offerings, and thy peace offerings, thy sheep, and thine oxen: in all places where I record my name I will come unto thee, and I will bless thee.

25 And if thou wilt make me an altar of stone, thou shalt not build it of hewn stone: for if thou lift up thy tool upon it, thou hast polluted it.

Our New Testament covenant has very similar rules. The place is selected by God, in the spirit (John 4:24). We are also instructed to assemble together (as many then and today chose to do their own thing). Our worship must be in truth. So, our belief system, doctrine and lifestyle must adhere to God's requirements.

John 4:24 (KJV)
God [is] a Spirit: and they that worship him must worship [him] in spirit and in truth.

LESSON 1

Worship and service goes together.

Luke 4:8 (KJV)
And Jesus answered and said unto him, Get thee behind me, Satan: for it is written, **Thou shalt worship the Lord thy God, and him only shalt thou serve.**

Service is never determined by the server. Servers serve. So, there must be instructions given first to the servant that must be followed. You do not get to decide how or in what capacity you will serve God. If you decide to feed the homeless or clothe a needy family that is not service to God. Working at your church or being a help to your pastor is not a service to God. That is sacrifice. In order for it to be a service, the Lord would have to tell you to do it. In following this command, order, and instruction from God you are now serving Him.

How you serve God is a part of worship. Your integrity, honesty, faithfulness, dedication, and commitment are a part of that equation. Also, the attitude in which the service is rendered matters. We are to serve the Lord with all our heart (1 Samuel 12:20); with fear (Psalms 2:11); with gladness (Psalms 100:2).

The sacrifice or offering is also determined by God. Romans 12:1 says to present your body as a living sacrifice. My body is no longer my own. We are to submit ourselves to God. Hebrews 13:15, we are to bring the fruit of lips, the sacrifice of praise. Our hearts must be engaged and not just our lips. Jesus said with the mouth we draw close to Him. With our lips we honor Him. But if your heart is far from Him, your worship will not be received.

When we thank God with our voice, that is also a sacrifice. Jonah 2:9 says, "I will sacrifice unto thee with the voice of thanksgiving…"

Our posture matters as well, whether we pray standing, seated, or prostrate, it makes a difference. The lifting of our hands (Psalms 141:2) and singing unto God are elements of worship.

Doing good for and to others is a sacrifice. Communicating is also a sacrifice. The word communicate means fellowship, community, and communion. Our fellowship (communication) with one another is a sacrifice to God. And He is pleased with both of these sacrifices.

Hebrews 13:16 (KJV)
But to do good and to communicate [fellowship] forget not: for with such sacrifices God is well pleased.

All of this is a part of our worship and service to God. There's more but I believe this provides insight.

4. Departing from evil

Job 28:28 (KJV)
*And unto man he said, Behold, the fear of the Lord, that [is] wisdom; and **to depart from evil** [is] understanding.*

The fear of the Lord is departing from evil. We are to shun (avoid, ignore, or reject) evil through antipathy or caution. We are not to engage in it. We must turn away from it. We should not even mentally entertain evil thoughts. Cain is our example as God instructed him to change his countenance and way of thinking.

Psalms 34 also explains what the fear of the Lord is. Departing from evil is on this list as well

5. Keep thy tongue from evil
6. Keep thy lips from speaking guile (telling lies/deceit)
7. Do good
8. Seek peace
9. Pursue peace

Psalms 34:11-14 (KJV)

11. Come, ye children, hearken unto me: I will teach you the fear of the LORD.

12. What man [is he that] desireth life, [and] loveth [many] days, that he may see good?

13. keep thy tongue from evil, and thy lips from speaking guile.

14. depart from evil, and do good; seek peace, and pursue it.

Psalms 34 explains several things we are to do and not do. The first is to keep our tongues from evil. We are to avoid speaking guile. This is the telling of lies or being deceitful. Some people feel it is okay to be deceitful and allow someone to "think whatever they want." But when a person is purposely being deceptive, this is lying. It is darkness. Small lies or white lies are still lies.

We are to do good, seek peace and pursue peace. When we are presented with the opportunity to do good, we must do good. If we chose not to do good when we have the means or ability to do so, it is a sin.

James 4:17 (NIV)

If anyone, then, knows the good they ought to do and doesn't do it, it is sin for them.

Luke 6:35 (KJV)
But love ye your enemies, and do good, and lend, hoping for nothing again; and your reward shall be great, and ye shall be the children of the Highest: **for he is kind unto the unthankful and to the evil.**

If God is kind to the unthankful and the evil, then what will He require of us as His children? We can not only do good to those that we like. We must do good because this is our nature. And this goodness is to be experienced by those that are unthankful and evil. It is the goodness of God that causes men to repent (Romans 2:4).

10. To hate evil

We are not to just shun and avoid evil, we are to hate it as well. We are to have the same attitude towards evil as God does. But evil is not overcome with more evil. It is overcome with good.

Romans 12:21 (NIV)
"Do not be overcome by evil, but overcome evil with good."

What is evil? Proverbs 8:13 provides us with a specific list of what evil is.

Proverbs 8:13 (KJV)
The fear of the LORD [is] to hate evil: pride, and arrogancy, and the evil way, and the froward mouth, do I hate.

- Pride
- Arrogance
- The evil way (evil behavior, conduct)
- Froward mouth (perverse mouth)

LESSON 1

Pride, arrogance, and the evil way are those that seek their own way. They are wise in their own eyes. They reject God's way.

Proverbs 3:7 (KJV)
Be not wise in thine own eyes: fear the LORD, and depart from evil.

Proverbs 3:7 defines evil as being wide in your own eyes. Pride is evil behavior in God's eyes. Egotistically, thinking you have the right answers will lead to an unwanted end. To consider yourself wise, and take a conceited approach is not the fear of the Lord. There is safety in counsel. **Proverbs 24:6** says, "But in the multitude of counsellors, there is safety." This does not mean I'm asking a bunch of people what they think I should do. The question is, what is the Lord saying you should do? The Lord many times speaks through others as you are searching for answers. We must be attentive to the voice of the Shepard.

Proverbs 14:16 (AMP)
A wise man suspects danger and cautiously avoids evil, But the fool is arrogant and careless.

A froward mouth is a person that is perverse, deceitful.

Let's take a look at what perverse means. Jesus was angry with the disciples and called them a "perverse generation" in Matthew 17:17. This word is found throughout the scriptures, and it is never connected to anything good. It is a characteristic that God really does not like.

Proverbs 28:18
*Whoso walketh uprightly shall be saved: but he that is **perverse** in his ways shall fall at once.*

Perverse has several definitions that are important in understanding this behavior.

Perverse:
- a) corrupt; turned away from what is right or good
- b) showing a deliberate and obstinate desire to behave in a way that is unreasonable or unacceptable, often in spite of the consequences.
- c) deliberately behaving badly or improperly, despite knowing that your actions are likely to have bad consequences.
- d) easily irritated or annoyed

God hates pride, arrogance, evil behavior and intent, and a froward (perverse) mouth, Proverbs 8:13.

11. Keep your word no matter the outcome, be honest and trustworthy

12. Do not take advantage or condemn others for profit

Psalm 15:3-5 (KJV)
3 He that backbiteth not with his tongue, nor doeth evil to his neighbour, nor taketh up a reproach against his neighbour.
4 In whose eyes a vile person is contemned; but **he honoureth them that fear the LORD. He that sweareth to his own hurt, and changeth not.**
5 He that putteth not out his money to usury, nor taketh reward against the innocent. He that doeth these things shall never be moved.

In Psalm 15, there are several things this passage tells us not to do. Do not backbite, do evil, or slander our neighbors. We are then told to honor those that fear the Lord. We are to put a value on those that fear God. Those that fear the Lord are those that will swear to their hurt and will not change. This means when you give your word, even if it puts you in a bad situation or causes you to lose out, keep your word. Keep your promise, keep your word, do not be a vow or oath breaker. It went on to explain, do not ask for interest when you allow someone to borrow money. Do not take bribes to testify against an innocent person. We must be truthful, trustworthy, and honest.

This is the fear of the Lord. The list outlines things we are to do and things we are to refrain from. Things that are displeasing to God and our attitude and response to these things as well.

1. Keep the Lord's commandments, statutes, ordinances, and precepts
2. Tithe
3. Worship and service
4. Depart from evil (evil: pride, arrogance, the evil way, a perverted and perverse mouth)
5. Do good
6. Seek peace
7. Pursue peace
8. Keep your tongue from evil
9. Do not lie (speaking guile)
10. Hate evil
11. Keep your word no matter the outcome, be honest and trustworthy
12. Do not take advantage or condemn others for profit

The fear of the Lord outlines for us our relationship with God. But the majority of the list deals with our attitudes and interaction with people. 70% of the list is about our conduct and the position of our hearts in our dealings with others. The fear of the Lord is mostly about relationship with people and the requirement to live an honest life of integrity.

Our real love, honor, and reverence for God are displayed in our relationship with others. We can not honor God and dishonor our brother or sister. We honor God through our worship, tithing, and obedience. But it is also displayed through our love towards others. We are to love the brotherhood (our sisters and brothers in the faith).

1 Peter 2:17 (KJV)
Honour all men. Love the brotherhood. Fear God. Honour the king.

CHAPTER 7

PETER TEACHES THE FEAR OF THE LORD

FEAR OF THE LORD

Apostle Peter teaches the fear of the Lord in his letter written to the church. It is a direct reference to Psalms 34:11-16.

Psalms 34:11-16 (KJV)
11 Come, ye children, hearken unto me: I will teach you the fear of the LORD.

12 What man [is he that] desireth life, [and] loveth [many] days, that he may see good?

13 Keep thy tongue from evil, and thy lips from speaking guile.

14 Depart from evil, and do good; seek peace, and pursue it.

15 The eyes of the LORD [are] upon the righteous, and his ears [are open] unto their cry.

16 The face of the LORD [is] against them that do evil, to cut off the remembrance of them from the earth.

Paul uses this passage to outline how those apart of the body of Christ must be towards each other. He explains that this way of life will produce life and good days.

1 Peter 3:8-12 (KJV)
8 Finally, [be ye] all of one mind, having compassion one of another, love as brethren, [be] pitiful, [be] courteous:

9 Not rendering evil for evil, or railing for railing: but contrariwise blessing; knowing that ye are thereunto called, that ye should inherit a blessing.

10 For he that will love life, and see good days, let him refrain his tongue from evil, and his lips that they speak no guile:

11 Let him eschew evil, and do good; let him seek peace, and ensue it.

12 For the eyes of the Lord [are] over the righteous, and his ears [are open] unto their prayers: but the face of the Lord [is] against them that do evil.

In this passage, Peter explains in detail the lifestyle and mindset of a person that walks in the fear of the Lord. He explains what is not acceptable and what the correct response and thinking must be.

In verse 12, Peter says the face of the Lord is against those that do evil. God is against those that are prideful, arrogant, choose to do evil (evil way), and have a froward mouth (perverse contrary people.) These are the type of behaviors God hates, Proverbs 8:13.

Peter explains in the last verse that the Lord watches over those that fear the Lord. And this lifestyle and way of life cause God's ears to be open to our prayers. The fear of the Lord affects our prayer life.

The Lord's prayer explains that we must forgive those who have trespassed against us. By not doing so, God will not forgive our trespasses and it affects our approach to God. 1 Peter 3:7 explained that a husband that does not honor his wife, will cause his prayers to be hindered. People think of prayer as being a conversation between them and God. But how we treat others directly affect our prayers. Walking in the fear of the Lord is critical to an effective prayer life. To be righteous first requires us to walk in godly fear.

1 Peter 3:12 (KJV)
For the eyes of the Lord [are] over the righteous, and his ears [are open] unto their prayers: but the face of the Lord [is] against them that do evil.

James 5:16 (KJV)

Confess [your] faults one to another, and pray one for another, that ye may be healed. ***The effectual fervent prayer of a righteous man availeth much.***

You cannot be righteous without walking in the fear of the Lord. James 5:16 is a scripture taught often as a standalone scripture. But the fear of God is the prerequisite to righteousness. We cannot treat people in ways that are displeasing to God and think our prayers will be effective.

CHAPTER 8

PAUL'S TEACHINGS ON THE GODLY FEAR

In Romans 3:10-18, Paul describes those that do not have the fear of the Lord. He quotes the book of Psalms. He begins with, "as it is written."

Romans 3:10-18 (KJV)

10 As it is written, There is none righteous, no, not one:

11 There is none that understandeth, there is none that seeketh after God.

12 They are all gone out of the way, they are together become unprofitable; there is none that doeth good, no, not one.

13 Their throat [is] an open sepulchre; with their tongues they have used deceit; the poison of asps [is] under their lips:

14 Whose mouth [is] full of cursing and bitterness:

15 Their feet [are] swift to shed blood:

16 Destruction and misery [are] in their ways:

17 And the way of peace have they not known:

18 There is no fear of God before their eyes.

Paul begins talking about righteousness. So, we see the connection between the fear of the Lord and righteousness. He says none have come into understanding. They are not seeking after God. They live life their own way and do not follow the ways of God. They are unprofitable. They may have earthly success, but spiritually, they are unprofitable. They are not serving God. They are serving themselves. No man can serve two masters. They will either serve God or mammon.

In verse 12, Paul says, "none do good." The fear of the Lord is to "do good". Paul then lists several behaviors that are contrary to the fear of the Lord. Their mouths produce death. Their mouths are deadly like a serpent and their words are deceitful (perverse). Everything out of their mouths is cursing and bitterness.

They are quick to shed blood. They're quick to cause death. Death is not always physical. They are quick to kill reputations, relationships, and dreams. They destroy people's lives with their actions. Everywhere they go, they leave destruction and produce misery. They have no peace, and their lives destroy peace wherever they go. They do not know the way of peace.

This description is of people that do not know the fear of the Lord. "There is no fear of God before their eyes." The fear of the Lord is to be careful with our mouths and our words. It is to seek and pursue peace. It's to shun evil. To do good and not evil. The people of God cannot be righteous and look like those described in Romans 3:10-18.

CHAPTER 9

LESSON 2

LESSON 2

The fear of the Lord is not just our list from Chapter 6: Lesson 1. There is a second part that is equally as important to the fear of the Lord.

There are several passages of scripture that connects the fear of the Lord to knowledge and wisdom.

Proverbs 1:7 (KJV)
The fear of the LORD [is] the beginning of knowledge: [but] fools despise wisdom and instruction.

Proverbs 1:29 (KJV)
For that they hated knowledge, and did not choose the fear of the LORD:

Proverbs 2:5 (KJV)
Then shalt thou understand the fear of the LORD, and find the knowledge of God.

Proverbs 9:10 (KJV)
The fear of the LORD [is] the beginning of wisdom: and the knowledge of the holy [is] understanding.

We have already looked at the fear of the Lord as it pertains to a relationship with God and the body of Christ. But another critical component of the fear of the Lord is its connection to knowledge and wisdom.

Proverbs 1:7 explains that the fear of the Lord is the first principle (step) of knowledge. Proverbs 9:10 says the fear of the Lord is the first principle (step) of wisdom. It is the first step. The knowledge and wisdom that comes from God cannot be obtained without living in the fear of the Lord.

Proverbs 1:7 explains that fools despise wisdom and instruction. They will hear wise counsel but choose not to listen. They will be given instructions and they won't listen. They do not fear the Lord. Proverbs 1:29 calls them people that hate knowledge. Those that fear the Lord follow instructions.

Proverbs 2:5 (KJV)
Then shalt thou understand the fear of the LORD, and find the knowledge of God.

Proverbs 2:5 says, "Then shalt thou understand the fear of the LORD." Notice the word "then." To practice a lifestyle of the fear of the Lord without understanding is not God's intent. The fear of the Lord brings us into covenant. It causes mysteries to be revealed. It gives us life, length of days, and protection. So, understanding the fear of the Lord is as important as adhering to the way of life.

Let's look at what was said before the word "then" so we can understand the fear of the Lord.

Proverbs 2:1-6 (KJV)
1 My son, if thou wilt receive my words, and hide my commandments with thee;
2 So that thou incline thine ear unto wisdom, [and] apply thine heart to understanding;
3 Yea, if thou criest after knowledge, [and] liftest up thy voice for understanding;

4 If thou seekest her as silver, and searchest for her as [for] hid treasures;

5 Then shalt thou understand the fear of the LORD, and find the knowledge of God.

6 For the LORD giveth wisdom: out of his mouth [cometh] knowledge and understanding.

The one speaking in this passage is the spirit of wisdom. We are given several instructions.

- Receive my words (seize, take in hand)
- Hide my commandments (hide, treasure, store up)
- Incline your ear unto wisdom (be attentive, pay attention)
- Apply your heart - understand (stretch out, extend)
- Cry after knowledge (call out, recite, cry out, proclaim)
- Lift up your voice for understanding
- Seek - (require, desire, request)
- Search (search out, search for, test)

When wisdom comes, we cannot be fools. We cannot despise it, ignore it, and throw it away. In Hosea 4:8, God said that His people are destroyed because of a lack of knowledge. But lack does not mean to be without. It does not mean if we have knowledge then God's people would not be destroyed. Lack means to be deficient. The standard is not where it should be.

Picture a first grader that takes a 3rd grade level test. They would be lost. Not because they lack knowledge but because they are not on that level and shouldn't be expected to do well on the test. But if a 3rd grader was given the 1st grade level test, the expectation is the 3rd grader should do well. There should be no areas of deficiencies. If there are, it raises concerns. Why can't the 3rd grader recognize their numbers? Where did the lack come from? Were they absent for a lengthy amount of time? Were they present but were not paying attention? Did they devalue the lesson and ignored it, thinking it wasn't important? In Hosea 4:6, the lack was a result of rejecting knowledge.

Hosea 4:6 (KJV)
My people are destroyed for lack of knowledge: **because thou hast rejected knowledge***, I will also reject thee, that thou shalt be no priest to me: seeing thou hast forgotten the law of thy God, I will also forget thy children.*

In Hosea 4, God had increased them. Because of this increase, they became prideful, so they began to reject the knowledge of God. The fear of the Lord is to hate pride and arrogance.

Hosea 4:7 (KJV)
As they were increased, so they sinned against me: [therefore] will I change their glory into shame.

We are instructed to receive words of wisdom. This means to take hold of that word or statement. When Godly knowledge comes, I must first recognize the Lord is speaking. And then, take hold of it. I remember it in an hour. I remember it at the end of the week. Next month and next year. I view the knowledge I received as valuable, so I held on to it to apply it when needs be.

To hide a commandment means it is in my heart and mind. I treat instructions as being valuable. I hold on to it like it is a treasure. It is how I govern my life and make decisions. It guides my moral compass.

Inclining your ear unto wisdom means we must hear wisdom when it comes. It comes in different ways. As we are looking to the Lord for what to do or how something is to be done or handled, the Lord will speak. But we have to recognize when He speaks. Our ears must be attentive. We must pay attention. Or the answer can come, and we completely miss it. Wisdom is action. Wisdom tells you how to achieve the goal.

Wisdom is the application of knowledge. Think of knowledge as being knowledgeable, you may understand cars and understand what may cause a car to overheat. Wisdom is applying knowledge. It is the correct response to the problem. Wisdom is not a guessing game. It is the best course of action, which may be to sell the car and not fix it at all.

Applying your heart to understand means you have received wisdom. You know what the Lord has said but you may not have the understanding yet. The Lord wants us to come to an understanding. Paul exhorts the church constantly to be not ignorant. We are not simply servants obeying orders, we must understand the orders that were given to us and why they were given. Understanding does not come without effort. We must press in. We must ask for an explanation and not be satisfied until we have obtained an understanding. Once the light bulb goes off, you have obtained an understanding. You have now become enlightened and now you can walk in the light. You can clearly see where to go, what to do, how to do it, why you are doing it, etc.

In our example of a car that broke down, understanding is knowing why you chose the course of action you did. It's understanding the other options and why you are going with the best option, which may not be the best option if you were someone else.

When it comes to the mysteries and secrets of God, applying your heart to understand means you search for understanding. And when you think you understand, you keep searching. You leave no rock unturned. Understanding is the concept of stretching out and extending. Understanding is growth. But this only occurs by knowledge being applied. Wisdom must be tested. Applying the heart takes time and it requires experience. Being right, in theory, is not applying the heart.

To cry after knowledge means your voice is raised. You are trying to obtain knowledge with everything in you. There's no shame holding you back from trying to get knowledge. This is a cry to heaven, putting a demand on heaven for knowledge and understanding.

This may also include no longer searching on your own. You are now talking to others. You're searching for confirmation and discrepancies. You're not looking to be right but you're searching for truth. Are there holes or errors in your conclusion? Are there things you hadn't considered? By talking to others, they will send you down other rabbit trails as you search for understanding and answers. Don't talk to those with no knowledge or understanding looking for validation and praise. Talk to those that can challenge or validate the conclusion because of their experience and education. This is lifting up your voice for understanding. This is seeking. This is searching out a matter. If your conclusion can not stand up to testing and constructive criticism, then you have not obtained wisdom or knowledge.

The end conclusion needs and must be the word of the Lord. The Lord will speak to those that are searching. "Those that seek me early shall find me," Proverbs 8:17. Early in this verse does not mean praying in the morning as many teach. It means to seek God for wisdom early in the process. Our search is to find out what the Lord says regarding the matter.

Only after this will you understand the fear of the Lord.

Proverbs 2:
5 Then shalt thou understand the fear of the LORD, and find the knowledge of God.
6 For the LORD giveth wisdom: out of his mouth [cometh] knowledge and understanding.

Verse 6 explains that the Lord gives wisdom, knowledge, and understanding, but it comes after you have done all 8 things on the list. Knowledge and wisdom do not just come to us. God does not magically download it to us. Revelation from God comes after you have knowledge, and you walk in wisdom. Only then will God explain something you did not understand because now you are knowledgeable about the subject. Jesus asked Nicodemus in essence, "how can we talk about spiritual things when you do not understand natural things?"

As we pursue answers and understanding, knowledge and wisdom will come. It comes in the search. We can't be afraid to be wrong or be challenged.

Luke 11:9 (KJV)
And I say unto you, Ask, and it shall be given you; seek, and ye shall find; knock, and it shall be opened unto you.

Ask and keep asking. Seek and search and search again. Knock and knock repeatedly until the door opens. This is how knowledge and wisdom are obtained.

This mindset and approach to wisdom, plus the mindset and conduct of godly fear is the full picture of the fear of the Lord. You cannot pursue one side of the coin and ignore the other. It is keeping God's commandments, shunning evil, but also the pursuit of knowledge, wisdom, and obtaining understanding.

Those that hate knowledge. They do not seek to learn and understand. They do not have the fear of the Lord.

Proverbs 1:29 (KJV)
For that they hated knowledge, and did not choose the fear of the LORD:

Proverbs 3:7 (KJV)
Be not wise in thine own eyes: fear the LORD, and depart from evil.

CHAPTER 10

THE BEGINNING OF KNOWLEDGE

Proverbs 1:7 (KJV)
The fear of the LORD [is] the beginning of knowledge: [but] fools despise wisdom and instruction.

Proverbs 9:10 (KJV)
The fear of the LORD [is] the beginning of wisdom: and the knowledge of the holy [is] understanding.

The fear of the Lord is the beginning of both knowledge and wisdom. Using the scriptures' explanation of what the fear of the Lord is, helps us see how it is the beginning of knowledge.

In order to have knowledge or walk in wisdom, God has required godly fear to be the first step. In the scriptures that reveal what the fear of the Lord is, we find two characteristics that rival knowledge and wisdom. These are pride and arrogance.

Proverbs 8:13 (KJV)
The fear of the LORD [is] to hate evil: **pride, and arrogancy**, *and the evil way, and the froward mouth, do I hate.*

Proverbs 1:7 explains the fear of the LORD is the beginning of knowledge. It is the fear of the Lord that causes us to understand God. "Knowledge of the holy [is] understanding," Proverbs 9:10. As we grow in our understanding of the fear of the Lord we grow in our understanding of "the Holy One" which is God.

The requirement is not simply to live in godly fear. The practice and lifestyle of it are not enough, we must come to an understanding. In this place, we have a full picture of the Father. We know what He is pleased with and what displeases Him.

The fear of the Lord is to hate pride. God calls pride evil. In Proverbs 16, Solomon lists the 7 things God hates. He calls them abominations. The first is a proud look.

Proverbs 6:16-17 (KJV)
16 *These six [things] doth the LORD hate: yea, seven [are] an abomination unto him:*
17 *A proud look…*

Pride is important. God made man to have pride. Pride is "reasonable or justifiable self-respect." It is also "delight or elation arising from some act, possession, or relationship," as defined by Webster Dictionary.

Parents take pride in their children when they play well at a recital or score in a sport. The glory of a father is when his child does well. God was so pleased with Jesus that He spoke from heaven voicing His pleasure. "This is my son in whom I am well pleased." The glory of God is Jesus Christ.

God instructs us to seek His kingdom and righteousness. But He also tells us to seek His glory.

Romans 2:7 (KJV)
To them who by patient continuance in well doing ***seek for glory and honour*** *and immortality, eternal life:*

God does not have an issue with pride. He has an issue with being prideful. To be prideful is to be disdainful or haughty.

Disdainful is "full of or expressing contempt for someone or something regarded as unworthy or inferior."

Haughty is "having or showing an attitude of superiority and contempt for people or things perceived to be inferior." In the scriptures, pride and haughty are mentioned together in Proverbs 16:18.

Proverbs 16:18 (KJV)
Pride [goeth] before destruction, and an haughty spirit before a fall.

Pride ends in destruction. A haughty spirit leads to people falling from grace. Whereas those that are humble are exalted and they receive honor.

Proverbs 15:33 (KJV)
The fear of the LORD [is] the instruction of wisdom; and **before honour [is] humility.**

Proverbs 15:33 explains that the system of honor begins with humility. We must be clothed in humility. If we humble ourselves under the mighty hand of God, He will exalt us in time. This is being lifted up into a position or onto a platform and honor is bestowed.

Pride causes a person's mind to be lifted up. Their minds are hardened. This is a mindset. Their mind is set, made up and they refuse to budge.

Daniel 5:20 (KJV)
But when his heart was lifted up, and his mind hardened in pride, he was deposed from his kingly throne, and they took his glory from him:

A hard heart is a person that refuses to listen. They have a "yeah but" response for every statement. They won't consider the opinions of others. They devalue others' expertise. They degrade others. They think they know and got it figured out.

But they are deceived. They will eventually fall. The platform that they've managed to build or given access to, they will eventually fall from and hit rock bottom (the ground).

Obadiah 1:3 (KJV)
The pride of thine heart hath deceived thee, thou that dwellest in the clefts of the rock, whose habitation [is] high; that saith in his heart, Who shall bring me down to the ground?

Those that are full of pride end up being ashamed. Where they were once glorified and honored, all they wear now is shame.

Proverbs 11:2 (KJV)
[When] pride cometh, then cometh shame: but with the lowly [is] wisdom.

We must remain lowly, humble. No matter how large the platform or high up the ladder one ascends, we must be clothed in humility. This is done by not being wise in your own eyes.

Proverbs 3:7 (KJV)
Be not wise in thine own eyes: fear the LORD, and depart from evil.

Proverbs 3:7 can easily read: be not wise in your own eyes, fear the Lord and depart from pride.

Isaiah 5:21 (KJV)
Woe unto [them that are] wise in their own eyes, and prudent (clever) in their own sight!

Rather than assuming and presuming we have the right answer, we are to search matters out. In all of our getting, get understanding. Presumption is very dangerous. I have seen many Christians presume that God will be with them or because they had faith that things would work out. Faith first requires a word from God. If God did not say it, then He is not obligated to perform it. Moses told the nation of Israel not to go into the promised land after God told them they would wander in the wilderness for forty years. Instead, they decided they were going to go in and take the land. Moses told them that he, Aaron, and the ark of the covenant was not going with them. The Israelites went and tried to take the land God had previously promised them but had changed His word regarding the matter after they had sinned and would not believe the word of Joshua and Caleb.

Numbers 14: (NIV)
43 For the Amalekites and the Canaanites will face you there. Because you have turned away from the LORD, he will not be with you and you will fall by the sword."
44 Nevertheless, in their presumption they went up toward the highest point in the hill country, though neither Moses nor the ark of the LORD's covenant moved from the camp.
45 Then the Amalekites and the Canaanites who lived in that hill country came down and attacked them and beat them down all the way to Hormah.

We must open our ears to hear wisdom, apply our hearts to understand, request help until we have insight and understanding. Only then do we find the knowledge we are searching for. Only then does God release His knowledge and gives us wisdom from above.

Proverbs 2:1-6 (NIV)
1 My son, if you accept my words and store up my commands within you,
2 turning your ear to wisdom and applying your heart to understanding--

3 indeed, if you call out for insight and cry aloud for understanding,

4 and if you look for it as for silver and search for it as for hidden treasure,

5 then you will understand the fear of the LORD and find the knowledge of God.

6 For the LORD gives wisdom; from his mouth come knowledge and understanding.

If we search for godly wisdom as outlined in the above scripture, God will release it. The Lord will reveal the correct path. The path(s) of righteousness. And it will be a path that sits well with your soul.

Psalm 23 (KJV)
1 The LORD is my shepherd; I shall not want.

2 He maketh me to lie down in green pastures: he leadeth me beside the still waters.

3 He restoreth my soul: he leadeth me in the paths of righteousness for his name's sake.

Proverbs 2:9-10 (NIV)
*9 Then you will understand what is right and just and fair--**every good path**.*

*10 For wisdom will enter your heart, and knowledge will be **pleasant to your soul**.*

You avoid being prideful by walking in humility and honor. Humility is lowering yourself and looking to God rather than self for the answer.

Matthew 23:12 (KJV)
And whosoever shall exalt himself shall be abased; and he that shall humble himself shall be exalted.

We are to look to God regarding every decision we make.

Proverbs 3:6 (KJV)
In all thy ways acknowledge him, and he shall direct thy paths.

You avoid being wise in your own eyes by taking counsel from others. Listening to others' advice and obtaining godly counsel. Valuing the experience, education, and expertise of others. Honor is placing value on others. In God's kingdom, honor is not earned. Honor must be given. We are to honor everyone. 1 Peter 2:17 tells us to "honor all men." By humbling ourselves and honoring others, it opens us up to hear the counsel and direction others have to give.

Proverbs 11:14 (KJV)
Where no counsel [is], the people fall: but in the multitude of counsellors [there is] safety.

I have often heard the Lord's answer to my problem as I have gone to others for advice. Some were not even aware the Lord was speaking through them, but they gave me the exact answer I needed.

Proverbs 22:4 (KJV)
By humility [and] the fear of the LORD [are] riches, and honour, and life.

Looking to God first for what is to be done is how David lived. He did not just make decisions. He sought God. David did not fight against Goliath without first consulting God. David told Goliath he was coming against him "in the name of the Lord." That means the Lord told him to go and He would grant him victory.

David was a man of war. He had seen many victories in battle. But he still consulted God first. He did not rely on his experience and expertise to figure out what to do. David was not wise in his own eyes. He always inquired of the Lord for direction.

In 2 Samuel, the Philistines came to fight against David. David inquired of the Lord what he should do.

2 Samuel 5:17-19 (KJV)
17 But when the Philistines heard that they had anointed David king over Israel, all the Philistines came up to seek David; and David heard [of it], and went down to the hold.

18 The Philistines also came and spread themselves in the valley of Rephaim.

19 And David enquired of the LORD, saying, Shall I go up to the Philistines? Wilt thou deliver them into mine hand? And the LORD said unto David, Go up: for I will doubtless deliver the Philistines into thine hand.

Immediately, following this victory, the Philistines came against David again. David did not assume, and he did not just follow the first instructions given by God. He did not presume God would grant him victory without first asking. He did not rely on his experience and expertise. Instead, David enquired of God a second time. And this time, rather than saying, "go up," God gave him very specific directions.

2 Samuel 5:22-25 (KJV)
22 And the Philistines came up yet again, and spread themselves in the valley of Rephaim.

23 And when David enquired of the LORD, he said, Thou shalt not go up; [but] fetch a compass behind them, and come upon them over against the mulberry trees.

24 And let it be, when thou hearest the sound of a going in the tops of the mulberry trees, that then thou shalt bestir thyself: for then shall the LORD go out before thee, to smite the host of the Philistines.

25 And David did so, as the LORD had commanded him; and smote the Philistines from Geba until thou come to Gazer.

The instructions might be different every time. God is not locked in. He does not have a set way of accomplishing what you need. He is the creator, and His creativity is unmatched.

Do not be wise in your own eyes and lifted up in pride. Be humble. Acknowledge God. And He will give you direction. His word will reveal what to do. This means keeping your ears open for the Lord to speak through others.

Proverbs 8:33 (KJV)
Hear instruction, and be wise, and refuse it not.

Proverbs 12:1 (KJV)
Whoso loveth instruction loveth knowledge: but he that hateth reproof [is] brutish.

Proverbs 12:1 (NIV)
Whoever loves discipline loves knowledge, but whoever hates correction is stupid.

CHAPTER 11

IF ANY LACK WISDOM

FEAR OF THE LORD

If the fear of the Lord is the beginning of wisdom, how does that truth reconcile with James 1:5. James said, "If any of us lack wisdom, we can ask God for it."

James 1:5 (KJV)
If any of you lack wisdom, let him ask of God, that giveth to all [men] liberally, and upbraideth not; and it shall be given him.

First, the fear of the Lord teaches us how to hear God's voice. We come into a place of understanding as we walk in godly fear. As we keep His commandments, depart from and hate evil, watch our mouths, do good, seek peace, walk in humility and honor, all of this creates an atmosphere conducive to God's presence. God's eyes and ears are attentive to those that fear Him.

Psalm 33:18 (KJV)

Behold, the eye of the LORD [is] upon them that fear him, upon them that hope in his mercy;

James 1:5 gives the impression that all we have to do is ask God for wisdom and it will be released to us. God will show us the way. He will grant us the know-how to navigate through our situation with success. However, James 1:5 is not a standalone scripture.

"If any of you lack wisdom..." Lack implies that there is a problem. There is a deficiency present. The word lack (*leipō*) means: to leave, leave behind, forsake, to be left behind. So, wisdom came already, and it was forsaken. It was either ignored altogether or left behind at some point in the journey. This mindset is what Jesus described as being thorny ground.

Mark 4:19 (KJV)
And the cares of this world, and the deceitfulness of riches, and the lusts of other things entering in, choke the word, and it becometh unfruitful.

A person that is thorny ground heard the word, they rejoiced but because of the busyness and business of life and the pursuit of wealth, the word was abandoned. The word was choked and did not produce. Mark 4 explains the third cause of a thorny ground mindset is lust.

James began the chapter by telling them to count it joy when they find themselves in "divers temptations."

James 1:2 (KJV)
My brethren, count it all joy when ye fall into divers temptations;

Temptation is a result of lust, the inward working of a strong desire for what is forbidden. So, if we know it is forbidden, why is there a struggle? If we keep the Lord's commandments, then whatever the Lord says is off-limits has to be off-limits no matter what.

As James further explains, a double-minded man is unstable.

James 1:8 (KJV)
A double-minded man [is] unstable in all his ways.

Before then, James talked about wavering back and forth.

James 1:6 (KJV)
But let him ask in faith, nothing wavering. For he that wavereth is like a wave of the sea driven with the wind and tossed.

This is the cause of the lack of wisdom. They were double-minded and wavering on what to do. So, James tells them God will send wisdom because they ignored or abandoned God's wisdom the first time around. This caused them to end up in this predicament.

James warns them that this temptation did not come from God. God does not tempt us with evil. This temptation comes from lust. Lust is an internal enticement. And if it is not dealt with and the path you are currently on is not forsaken, the end result will be death. Lust produces sinful actions, and sinful actions lead to death. James explains this a few verses later.

James 1:14-15 (KJV)
14 *But every man is tempted, when he is drawn away of his own lust, and enticed.*

15 *Then when lust hath conceived, it bringeth forth sin: and sin, when it is finished, bringeth forth death.*

James tells them to repent, which means to change direction. Repentance is to change one's mind for the better. He tells them to get rid of the filth and the evil in their lives. They must humble themselves and receive God's word (God's wisdom) which was sent to save them.

James 1:21 (NLT)
So get rid of all the filth and evil in your lives, and humbly accept the word God has planted in your hearts, for it has the power to save your souls.

James 1:22 (KJV)
But be ye doers of the word, and not hearers only, deceiving your own selves.

If they had been a doer of the word and not only a hearer, they would not be lacking in wisdom. By not following the instructions, they deceived themselves. Pride deceives. They wavered, they were double-minded and chose their way forsaking the wisdom of God.

In order to ask for wisdom according to James 1:5, we must first fear the Lord. This is turning from pride and walking in humility. Getting rid of filth and evil ways. Deciding not to be unstable and follow the Lord's plan. Only by getting back on the path of righteousness can we avoid the outcome our lust is now producing. We must depart from evil and keep (to) God's way. This will keep us from regret and heartbreak.

Proverbs 16:17 (KJV)
The highway of the upright [is] to depart from evil: he that keepeth his way preserveth his soul.

CHAPTER 12

THE MIND OF A KING

1 Peter 2:9 (KJV)
But ye [are] a chosen generation, a royal priesthood, an holy nation, a peculiar people; that ye should shew forth the praises of him who hath called you out of darkness into his marvellous light:

Peter refers to the body of Christ as a chosen generation, a royal priesthood. Royal deals with kingship. When God established the kingship in Israel, the kings were required to write out their own book of the law. They hand wrote the 613 laws of Moses. David's last words talked about the fear of the Lord. Kings are experts. They were experts in the law, trade (imports and exports), their nation's economy and economics, the military, history, education, politics, and so many other areas that are needed to run a successful kingdom.

Kings that were prideful always fell.

Proverbs 16:18 (KJV)
Pride [goeth] before destruction, and an haughty spirit before a fall.

The fear of the Lord requires us to depart from pride. Kings surrounded themselves with counselors. They understood their success was not about being the smartest person in the room, it was about making the right decision.

King Saul had one of the most important prophets in the scriptures at his disposal. Samuel was a judge, a priest, and a prophet. He was given to open visions (1 Samuel 3:1).

1 Samuel 7:15 (KJV)
*And **Samuel judged Israel** all the days of his life.*

1 Samuel 10:8 (KJV)
*And thou shalt go down before me to Gilgal; and, behold, I will come down unto thee, to **offer burnt offerings, [and] to sacrifice sacrifices of peace offerings**: seven days shalt thou tarry, till I come to thee, and shew thee what thou shalt do.*

1 Samuel 3:20 (KJV)
*And all Israel from Dan even to Beersheba knew that **Samuel [was] established [to be] a prophet of the LORD**.*

Samuel's words never fell to the ground. This means everything he spoke came to pass. His prophecies were never wrong.

1 Samuel 3:19 (KJV)
And Samuel grew, and the LORD was with him, and did let none of his words fall to the ground.

However, Saul would not listen. He did not follow the instructions given to him by Samuel. Samuel, as a prophet, was the mouthpiece of God. So, Saul was really rejecting God's word and not Samuel's. Saul was both prideful and insecure. He was a people pleaser. And this cost him his kingdom.

God tried to fix Saul's insecurities before he became king. God chose Saul because he was head and shoulders above his brethren. Saul was superior to his peers. He had kingly qualities. But he still had insecurities. So, with his first encounter with Samuel, God tried to fix Saul's mind. God tried to change how Saul viewed himself and build him up. God addressed Saul's insecurities through the prophet.

1 Samuel 9:22-26 (KJV)

22 And Samuel took Saul and his servant, and brought them into the parlour, and made them sit in the chiefest place among them that were bidden, which [were] about thirty persons.

23 And Samuel said unto the cook, Bring the portion which I gave thee, of which I said unto thee, Set it by thee.

24 And the cook took up the shoulder, and [that] which [was] upon it, and set [it] before Saul. And [Samuel] said, Behold that which is left! set [it] before thee, [and] eat: for unto this time hath it been kept for thee since I said, I have invited the people. So Saul did eat with Samuel that day.

25 And when they were come down from the high place into the city, [Samuel] communed with Saul upon the top of the house.

26 And they arose early: and it came to pass about the spring of the day, that Samuel called Saul to the top of the house, saying, Up, that I may send thee away. And Saul arose, and they went out both of them, he and Samuel, abroad.

Saul was brought into the "parlour." He was given the chief seat (the head of the table) among the 30 people present. He was given the best portion of meat. He ate and broke bread with a national prophet, Samuel. They were in the "high place." Samuel talked to Saul on the "top of the house." All of these acts were prophetic and should have shifted Saul's thinking. Not to be prideful but in building him up. Saul needed confidence. Notice Saul's description of himself. This statement revealed how Saul viewed not only himself but his tribe and his family.

1 Samuel 9:21 (KJV)

And Saul answered and said, [Am] not I a Benjamite, of the smallest of the tribes of Israel? and my family the least of all the families of the tribe of Benjamin? wherefore then speakest thou so to me?

Saul was from the smallest tribe. And he was from the least family in the tribe. Saul saw himself as the least in the entire kingdom. God was exalting and elevating him, but Saul's mind never adjusted.

Saul would not tell his uncle about his encounter with Samuel when he returned home. And at this point, Saul had already been anointed to be king and captain.

1 Samuel 10:1 (KJV)
Then Samuel took a vial of oil, and poured [it] upon his head, and kissed him, and said, [Is it] not because the LORD hath anointed thee [to be] captain over his inheritance?

1 Samuel 10:16 (KJV)
And Saul said unto his uncle, He told us plainly that the asses were found. But of the matter of the kingdom, whereof Samuel spake, **he told him not.**

When Saul was presented to the nation to be king, he went and hid himself. God supernaturally revealed to Samuel where Saul was.

1 Samuel 10:22-23 (KJV)
22 Therefore they enquired of the LORD further, if the man should yet come thither. And the LORD answered, Behold, he hath hid himself among the stuff.
23 And they ran and fetched him thence: and when he stood among the people, he was higher than any of the people from his shoulders and upward.

Saul hid himself. He was concerned about people's perception of him. And he ran the nation with this mentality. Rather than pleasing God, it was more important for him to please men.

Proverbs 29:25 (KJV)

The fear of man bringeth a snare: but whoso putteth his trust in the LORD shall be safe.

Saul tried to obey God his way rather than being obedient to God. His walk was constantly compromised because of his insecurities. God eventually rejected Saul for his rebellious heart.

1 Samuel 15:22-23 (KJV)

22 *And Samuel said, Hath the LORD [as great] delight in burnt offerings and sacrifices, as in obeying the voice of the LORD? Behold, to obey [is] better than sacrifice, [and] to hearken than the fat of rams.*

23 *For rebellion [is as] the sin of witchcraft, and stubbornness [is as] iniquity and idolatry. Because thou hast rejected the word of the LORD, he hath also rejected thee from [being] king.*

Saul was anointed, but the anointing does not fix character flaws. One purpose of the anointing is to break the yoke. The anointing does not fix the vessel's insecurities. The encounter with Samuel before being anointed to be king should have elevated Saul's esteem, but it did not. Saul had no understanding of each prophetic act. He missed the statement God made concerning him. Unlike Gideon, who was called a "mighty man of valor" while hiding out, Gideon embraced those words spoken to him by the angel and it changed how he saw himself. This ultimately allowed him to complete the assignment God had called him to do as a judge over the nation of Israel.

Saul left Samuel the same way he was when he arrived and ruled the nation as an insecure man. God even changed Saul's heart. But that change allowed him to rule the nation, it did not change how Saul saw himself. You can see Saul's insecurities once David came on the scene.

David's success in battle led to a national song being written about his exploits. But Saul viewed it as a diss record. And it revealed his insecurities once again.

1 Samuel 18:8 (KJV)
And Saul was very wroth, and the saying displeased him; and he said, They have ascribed unto David ten thousands, and to me they have ascribed [but] thousands: and [what] can he have more but the kingdom?

Compare David to Saul. David was a wise man. Three times David is described as behaving wisely in 1 Samuel 18. In 2 Samuel 14:20, a woman described David as being wise and having the wisdom of an angel to know all things "in the earth."

2 Samuel 14:20 (KJV)
To fetch about this form of speech hath thy servant Joab done this thing: and **my lord [is] wise, according to the wisdom of an angel of God, to know all [things] that [are] in the earth.**

But he surrounded himself with prophets, counselors, and wise men. David was not insecure. Yet he listened to counsel. David did not have to be the smartest man in the room.

Look at some of the men that David was surrounded by:

Ahithophel the counselor

2 Samuel 15:12
And Absalom sent for Ahithophel the Gilonite, David's counsellor...

Ahithophel was not a prophet but like Samuel, his counsel never fell to the ground. He was always right. He eventually sided with Absalom against David. He later hung himself after Absalom did not listen to his counsel. Some teach Ahithophel hung himself because his counsel was rejected. I believe Ahithophel knew David was going to survive the coup and kill everyone that was part of the conspiracy. When Absalom did not listen, he knew the end had come. Knowing the prophecy Nathan spoke to David after he had Uriah killed, Ahithophel's counsel to Absalom proved instrumental in those words (prophecy) coming to pass.

Zadok the priest and seer

2 Samuel 15:27 (KJV)
The king said also unto Zadok the priest, [Art not] thou a seer? return into the city in peace, and your two sons with you, Ahimaaz thy son, and Jonathan the son of Abiathar.

Abiathar the priest

2 Samuel 15:27, 35
Hushai, the companion of David

He was instrumental in causing the conspiracy of Absalom to fail. His counsel was chosen over Ahithophel's.

1 Chronicles 27:33 (KJV)
And Ahithophel [was] the king's counsellor: and Hushai the Archite [was] the king's companion:

Gad, the prophet and David's seer

2 Samuel 24:11 (KJV)
For when David was up in the morning, the word of the LORD came unto the prophet Gad, David's seer, saying,

Nathan the prophet

2 Samuel 12:25 (KJV)
And he sent by the hand of Nathan the prophet; and he called his name Jedidiah, because of the LORD.

Jonathan, David's uncle

Jonathan was a counselor, a wise man, and a scribe.

1 Chronicles 27:32 (KJV)
Also Jonathan David's uncle was a counsellor, a wise man, and a scribe: and Jehiel the son of Hachmoni [was] with the king's sons:

David was surrounded by wise counsel. There may be more names, but I believe this paints a drastically different picture than the life of Saul. The fear of the Lord is to follow instructions.

Zephaniah 3:7 (KJV)
"I said, Surely thou wilt fear me, thou wilt receive instruction; so their dwelling should not be cut off..."

Saul followed the counsel of the people. But David surrounded himself with those that could hear God's voice. And yet, David was a man given to searching out knowledge and wisdom.

We have always highlighted David as a man of worship. But David also searched for understanding. He sought answers and knowledge. He constantly prayed, "Lord teach me thy ways."

Psalm 25:4 (KJV)
Shew me thy ways, O LORD; teach me thy paths.

Psalm 119:15 (KJV)
I will meditate in thy precepts, and have respect unto thy ways.

King David was teachable. He received counsel and followed instructions.

The mindset of a king is also one given to understand mysteries. They search for understanding.

Proverbs 25:2 (KJV)
[It is] the glory of God to conceal a thing: but the honour of kings [is] **to search out a matter**.

There are things that God has covered and concealed. He is waiting for a person with a kingly mindset to search out these mysteries. These mysteries will only be revealed to those who search and refuse to be satisfied until they have come to an understanding.

Proverbs 4:7 (HNV)
Wisdom is supreme. Get wisdom. Yes, though it costs all your possessions, get understanding.

The Lord desires that His people seek after him with all their hearts. There are mysteries and secrets the Lord wants to show them so that the world can be blessed by their findings. But there has to be a willingness to get an understanding. As a person comes into understanding, they really become an expert in that area. It becomes their area of expertise and renown. They become "known" for that area of discovery. This is where our prosperity lies, in our "field" of studies and expertise as the Lord reveals what had been concealed to the world. These are those whom God places His glory (weight) on. They are masters of their craft.

Romans 2:7 (KJV)
To them who by patient continuance in well doing seek for glory and honour and immortality, eternal life:

CHAPTER 13

FOR THEM THAT FEAR HIM

FEAR OF THE LORD

The fear of the Lord is the first principle. That means it is the foundation. It is a main ingredient or component to all the ways of God, from worship, holiness, service, righteousness, and more. It is like basic training in the military before soldiers are sent to be trained in their areas of expertise. It conditions Christians for lifestyle and service: physically, mentally, and emotionally.

Below is a list of things the fear of the Lord opens up to the people of God.

The secrets of God are reserved for those that fear Him.

God also only enters into a covenant with those that fear Him.

Psalm 25:14 (KJV)
*The **secret** of the LORD [is] with them that fear him; and he will shew them his **covenant**.*

There is divine protection for those that fear Him. The angels as released on their behalf and also brings deliverance.

Psalm 34:7 (KJV)
*The **angel of the LORD encampeth** round about them that fear him, and delivereth them.*

Many quote Psalms 23, "the Lord is my shepherd, I shall not want." But Jesus is not our shepherd just because of the prayer of salvation. Sheep obey and they follow. Those that fear the Lord have no want. The shepherd takes care of them.

Psalms 34:9 (KJV)
*O fear the LORD, ye his saints: for [there is] **no want** to them that fear him.*

Those that walk-in humility and the fear of the Lord experience its reward or results. The fear of the Lord produces riches, honor, and life.

Proverbs 22:4 (KJV)
By humility [and] the fear of the LORD [are] **riches, and honour, and life.**

Proverbs 22:4 (HNV)
The result of humility and the fear of the LORD Is **wealth, honor, and life.**

Proverbs 22:4 (ASV)
The reward of humility and the fear of Jehovah Is **riches, and honor, and life.**

Proverbs 22:4 (NIV)
Humility is the fear of the LORD; **its wages** are riches and honor and life.

Those that fear the Lord are secure, strong, and confident. They have strong hope.

Proverbs 14:26-27 (KJV)
26 *In the fear of the LORD [is] strong confidence: and his children shall have a place of refuge.*

Proverbs 14:26 (NIV)
Whoever fears the LORD has a secure fortress, and for their children it will be a refuge.

FEAR OF THE LORD

Proverbs 14:27
The fear of the LORD [is] a fountain of life, to depart from the snares of death.

The fountain of life is found for those that fear the Lord. Jesus said that He came to give us life and life more abundantly. Only through the fear of the Lord can we taste this promise. The word fountain is *māqôr* which means spring or source. Our life source begins with godly fear.

As a member of the body of Christ, we are required to submit ourselves to one another. But this submission must be done in the fear of the Lord. The fear of the Lord reveals to us the mindset the body must have towards one another. Submission cannot be fully accomplished without the fear of the Lord.

Ephesians 5:21 (KJV)
Submitting yourselves one to another in the fear of God.

The church is described in Acts 9:31 as walking in the fear of the Lord. Edification, comfort of the Holy Ghost, and the fear of the Lord cause the church to experience multiplication.

Acts 9:31 (KJV)
Then had the churches rest throughout all Judaea and Galilee and Samaria, and were edified; and walking in the fear of the Lord, and in the comfort of the Holy Ghost, were multiplied.

Holiness is perfect (brought to the place of maturity) when we fear the Lord. Holiness is not just what we don't do with our minds and body. It's also what we do and the things we entertain our minds with.

2 Corinthians 7:1 (KJV)
Having therefore these promises, dearly beloved, let us cleanse ourselves from all filthiness of the flesh and spirit, perfecting holiness in the fear of God.

Holiness also includes how we treat others. Paul explains true holiness in Ephesians 4. Notice his description of holiness. Most only think of things we are to refrain from like adultery, fornication, lying, lasciviousness, pride, and other behaviors God is not pleased with. But notice Paul explains how we are to be towards one another.

Ephesians 4: (KJV)
24 *And that ye put on the new man, which after God is created in righteousness and true holiness.*
25 *Wherefore putting away lying, speak every man truth with his neighbour: for we are members one of another.*
26 *Be ye angry, and sin not: let not the sun go down upon your wrath:*
27 *Neither give place to the devil.*
28 *Let him that stole steal no more: but rather let him labour, working with [his] hands the thing which is good, that he may have to give to him that needeth.*
29 *Let no corrupt communication proceed out of your mouth, but that which is good to the use of edifying, that it may minister grace unto the hearers.*
30 *And grieve not the holy Spirit of God, whereby ye are sealed unto the day of redemption.*
31 *Let all bitterness, and wrath, and anger, and clamour, and evil speaking, be put away from you, with all malice:*

32 And be ye kind one to another, tenderhearted, forgiving one another, even as God for Christ's sake hath forgiven you.

Our worship of God must be in the fear of the Lord. Worship is not just praise and adoration to God. Worship is a lifestyle and it includes our obedience to God, our service to Him, and our interaction with others.

Psalm 5:7 (KJV)
But as for me, I will come [into] thy house in the multitude of thy mercy: [and] in thy fear will I worship toward thy holy temple.

Our service to God must be done in the fear of the Lord. We are to reverence the Lord in and through our service. No matter what assignments God has given us, or place of authority, we must maintain the lifestyle and mindset of godly fear. As David explained in his final words, those that rule must do so in the fear of the Lord.

Deuteronomy 6:13 (KJV)
Thou shalt fear the LORD thy God, and serve him, and shalt swear by his name.

Prolonged days are connected to the fear of the Lord. Those that walk in godly fear have their days lengthened.

Proverbs 10:27 (KJV)

The fear of the LORD prolongeth days: but the years of the wicked shall be shortened.

CHAPTER 14

GODLY FEAR

FEAR OF THE LORD

Let's put lesson 1 and lesson 2 together so we can see the complete picture of what the fear of the Lord is.

Psalm 86:11 (KJV)
Teach me thy way, O LORD; I will walk in thy truth: unite my heart to fear thy name.

LESSON 1 (Chapter 6):

The fear of the Lord is:

1. Keep the Lord's commandments, statutes, and ordinances
2. Worship and service
3. Tithe
4. Do good
5. Seek peace
6. Pursue peace
7. Keep your tongue from evil
8. Do not lie
9. Depart from evil (evil: pride, arrogance, the evil way, a perverted and perverse mouth)
10. Hate evil
11. Keep your word no matter the outcome, be honest and trustworthy
12. Do not take advantage or condemn others for profit

LESSON 2 (Chapter 9):

The fear of the Lord is pursuit for wisdom and knowledge.

Proverbs 1:29 (KJV)
For that <u>they hated knowledge</u>, and did not choose the fear of the LORD:

Proverbs 3:7 (KJV)
<u>Be not wise in thine own eyes</u>: fear the LORD, and depart from evil.

1. Receive my words (seize, take in hand)
2. Hide my commandments (hide, treasure, store up)
3. Incline your ear - wisdom (be attentive, pay attention)
4. Apply your heart - understand (stretch out, extend)
5. Cry after knowledge (call out, recite, cry out, proclaim)
6. Lift up your voice for understanding
7. Seek - (require, desire, request)
8. Search (search out, search for, test)

Live a life that is pleasing to the Lord. Walk in the fear of the Lord.

Psalm 147:11 (KJV)
The LORD taketh pleasure in them that fear him*, in those that hope in his mercy.*

CHAPTER 15

LEARN TO FEAR

In looking at the full picture of what the fear of the Lord is, we see that godly fear is about mindsets and behavior. It is behavior that is pleasing to the Lord and behavior He does not like. It deals with our relationship with God and our relationship with others. You may think to live a life of godly fear requires self-control and self-effort.

Romans 6:12 (NLT)
Do not let sin control the way you live; do not give in to sinful desires.

Most sermons on sin leave the listeners believing to live a life of holiness, a life pleasing to the Lord, requires temperance and inner strength. But holiness and godly fear is not accomplished through human strength and effort.

If men could live a life of righteousness in their own strength, then there would have been no need for the Holy Spirit. Jesus' death would not have been required. The law of Moses proved that man could not live a sinless life even when man was aware of what God required.

In Romans 7, Paul describes in detail man's struggle to not sin. He highlights the desire to live a life pleasing to God but the war of the mind makes it difficult.

Romans 7:14-25 (NLT)
14 So the trouble is not with the law, for it is spiritual and good. The trouble is with me, for I am all too human, a slave to sin.
15 I don't really understand myself, for I want to do what is right, but I don't do it. Instead, I do what I hate.
16 But if I know that what I am doing is wrong, this shows that I agree that the law is good.

17 So I am not the one doing wrong; it is sin living in me that does it.

18 And I know that nothing good lives in me, that is, in my sinful nature. I want to do what is right, but I can't.

19 I want to do what is good, but I don't. I don't want to do what is wrong, but I do it anyway. 20 But if I do what I don't want to do, I am not really the one doing wrong; it is sin living in me that does it.

21 I have discovered this principle of life--that when I want to do what is right, I inevitably do what is wrong.

22 I love God's law with all my heart.

23 But there is another power within me that is at war with my mind. This power makes me a slave to the sin that is still within me.

24 Oh, what a miserable person I am! Who will free me from this life that is dominated by sin and death?

25 Thank God! The answer is in Jesus Christ our Lord. So you see how it is: In my mind I really want to obey God's law, but because of my sinful nature I am a slave to sin.

Paul provides the solution to this problem in Romans 8. If we live according to the flesh, we will continue to struggle with sin. We are instead to live a life according to the Spirit.

Living a life in the fear of the Lord cannot be accomplished in the flesh. To live a life by a checklist will eventually lead to frustration. It is really a legalistic approach to religion. It is human willpower. Legalism, which is trying to live by the letter, kills. It does not produce life, it produces death. It is the Spirit of God that gives life.

2 Corinthians 3:6 (NIV)
*He has made us competent as ministers of a new covenant--not of the letter but of the Spirit; for **the letter kills, but the Spirit gives life.***

Zechariah 4:6 (NIV)
So he said to me, "This is the word of the LORD to Zerubbabel:
'Not by might nor by power, but by my Spirit,' says the LORD Almighty.

A caterpillar cannot decide one day to be a butterfly. The caterpillar cannot change its thinking and in doing so, be a butterfly. A butterfly is an insect that went through a metamorphosis.

Romans 12:2 (KJV)
And be not conformed to this world: but be ye transformed by the renewing of your mind, that ye may prove what is that good, and acceptable, and perfect, will of God.

The phrase "be ye transformed" in Romans 12:2 comes from the word *metamorphoō*. Metamophosis is an abrupt developmental change. We must experience a change achieved by supernatural means. It is a change that occurs from the inside out. And the outward change is evident.

Many teach this passage in Romans to mean that we are changed by reading our Bibles. This is not accurate. Our minds are not changed by reading or memorizing scriptures. There was no Bible when this passage was written. We were not to replace the Old Testament with the New Testament in our approach to being righteous. It is not by work and effort on our part. We are transformed by the Holy Spirit and discipleship.

Trying to live a life of godly fear with our own effort and strength is an outward effort. It's thinking of the correct response rather than the natural response being the correct response. Our nature must be changed. A butterfly cannot decide to be a caterpillar or a butterfly, it can only be a butterfly because that's what it has become.

Psalms 34:11 (KJV)
Come, ye children, hearken unto me: I will teach you the fear of the LORD.

Only through teaching do we learn to fear the Lord. This word teach is *lāmad*. It means to learn, be trained, exercise in, expert. Having knowledge does not make you an expert. It is through exercising that a person becomes trained. Repetition and discipline are important components. To be trained means you have experienced and received correction and training.

Proverbs 15:10 (NIV)
Stern discipline awaits anyone who leaves the path; the one who hates correction will die.

Proverbs 12:1 (NIV)
Whoever loves discipline loves knowledge, but whoever hates correction is stupid.

Allowing yourself to be taught, trained, and corrected is what teaches you the fear of the Lord. The fathers taught it to their sons and the son's sons (Deuteronomy 6:2). The parents are to teach it to their children.

Ephesians 6:4 (KJV)
And, ye fathers, provoke not your children to wrath: but bring them up in the nurture and admonition of the Lord.

Ephesians 6:4 (BBE)
And, you fathers, do not make your children angry: but give them training in the teaching and fear of the Lord.

Proverbs 22:6 (KJV)
Train up a child in the way he should go: and when he is old, he will not depart from it.

Nowadays, teachings on fearing the Lord may not come from mom or dad. This was a requirement for the Israelites whose laws defined their culture and ways of life. Nowadays, this teaching may come from one of the five-fold ministries (apostles, prophets, teachers, pastors, and evangelists.) Possibly, an elder or bishop in the faith, a spiritual mother or father, or a mature saint in the Lord.

The second part is teaching comes through fellowship with the Father. The heavenly Father instructs those that fear Him in the way they are to go.

Psalms 25:12 (NIV)
Who, then, are those who fear the LORD? He will instruct them in the ways they should choose.

This means just as we submitted ourselves to our parents, and others that instruct us in godly fear, we are to follow the voice of God just the same. Receive the correction from God. Repent (change your thinking for the better) and embrace the adjustments. When correction comes, we must let go of the old way and the previous way of thinking and take hold of the new. To walk in godly fear does not require human effort. It requires obedience and understanding. The Holy Spirit was sent to guide us into all truth, and to "shew" us what is to come (John 16:13). We must live in the Spirit, walk in the Spirit, and be led by the Spirit of God.

Galatians 5:25 (NLT)
Since we are living by the Spirit, let us follow the Spirit's leading in every part of our lives.

Obedience and being fully agreeable to the instructions of man and the instructs from God produce the lifestyle and mindset of the fear of the Lord. Paul explains this combination in Hebrews 12.

Hebrews 12: (NIV)
5 And have you completely forgotten this word of encouragement that addresses you as a father addresses his son? It says, "My son, do not make light of the Lord's discipline, and do not lose heart when he rebukes you,

6 because the Lord disciplines the one he loves, and he chastens everyone he accepts as his son."

7 Endure hardship as discipline; God is treating you as his children. For what children are not disciplined by their father?

8 If you are not disciplined--and everyone undergoes discipline--then you are not legitimate, not true sons and daughters at all. 9 Moreover, we have all had human fathers who disciplined us and we respected them for it. How much more should we submit to the Father of spirits and live!

10 They disciplined us for a little while as they thought best; but God disciplines us for our good, in order that we may share in his holiness.

11 *No discipline seems pleasant at the time, but painful. Later on, however, it produces a harvest of righteousness and peace for those who have been trained by it.*

Verse 7 exhorts us to "endure hardship." The King James Version uses the word "endure chastening." This word is *paideia*. This word means: tutorage, education or training; disciplinary correction:—chastening, chastisement, instruction, nurture.

The concordance defines chastening [*paideia*] as the following…

- **A.** the whole training and education of children (which relates to the cultivation of mind and morals, and employs for this purpose now commands and admonitions, now reproof and punishment). It also includes the training and care of the body.
- **B.** whatever in adults also cultivates the soul, esp. by correcting mistakes and curbing passions.
  1. instruction which aims at increasing **virtue**
  2. chastisement, chastening, (of the evils with which God visits men for their amendment)

The end goal is virtue. Virtue is moral goodness, moral excellence, modesty, and purity. This is what it looks like to fear the Lord. This word virtue is *aretē*. It means moral goodness or moral excellence.

We are God's chosen people. When people see us and have experiences with us, their experience should feel like an encounter with our Heavenly Father. We are partakers of His divine nature. And this nature is developed in the fear of the living God. The fear of the Lord is what allows us to escape the corruption of this world. It addresses the heart, mind, and inner workings of man.

2 Peter 1:4-5 (KJV)
4 Whereby are given unto us exceeding great and precious promises: that by these ye might be partakers of the divine nature, having escaped the corruption that is in the world through lust.

5 And beside this, giving all diligence, **add to your faith <u>virtue</u>; and to <u>virtue</u> knowledge;**

This word virtue is *aretē*. It is the same word used in 1 Peter 2:9 for "praises."

1 Peter 2:9 (KJV)
But ye [are] a chosen generation, a royal priesthood, an holy nation, a peculiar people; that ye should shew forth the **<u>praises</u>** *of him who hath called you out of darkness into his marvellous light:*

We are God's chosen people, and it must be evident in the lives of those that fear Him. We "shew", not verbalize, the praises of God who brought us out of the kingdom of darkness. We cannot be those that vocalize praise and have outward expressions of praise to God but are evil towards our fellow man. We cannot honor God with our lips, but our hearts be far from Him. Only by walking in the fear of the Lord can God be glorified.

2 Corinthians 7:1 (KJV)
Having therefore these promises, dearly beloved, let us cleanse ourselves from all filthiness of the flesh and spirit, perfecting holiness in the fear of God.

www.ingramcontent.com/pod-product-compliance
Lightning Source LLC
Chambersburg PA
CBHW041146110526
44590CB00027B/4147